THE
SIDE
DISH
HANDBOOK

TORI RITCHIE

Photographs by
KATIE NEWBURN

Illustrations by
MARGARET BERG

weldon**owen**

CONTENTS

Why Side Dishes?

Next time you are at a restaurant, take a close look at your plate. You may have ordered meat or seafood, but the most interesting thing could be what comes with it. In this era of celebrating (even worshipping) the seasonal, sustainable, and local, side dishes often nudge out protein for the spotlight. It's here that chefs and home cooks explore their creativity, working with an unlimited palette of colors, textures, and flavors. You see the seeds of it when you wander the farmers' market. Watch people stopping to ogle the asparagus and stare at the bright orange cauliflower cultivar aptly named Cheddar. Isn't this where you find inspiration, too?

It's also where you are going to find maximum value and nutrition. Vegetables and grains are superfoods, full of vitamins, minerals, fiber, and antioxidants. The more you eat of them, the better you will feel. Plus, when you compare them to animal protein, plant foods are much more economical, and the cultivation and consumption of them is far better for the planet.

But this is not a book about health or economics or saving the environment. This is a book about unforgettable side dishes. These recipes zero in on forty vegetables and grains and the best way to serve them. Sometimes it is a spin on a classic recipe with an unexpected ingredient that makes it stand apart. Other times, the magic factor is the cooking method. If you grew up eating steamed brussels sprouts, no wonder you don't like them. If you roast them and serve them with bacon-walnut vinaigrette, no doubt your opinion will change.

Most of the recipes in this book are designed to serve four to six people for an everyday meal. They are simple dishes you can throw together at the end of the workday, then pair with a steak or chop (see page 92 for pairing suggestions). Almost all of the recipes can be doubled (or more) to feed a crowd, and several are great choices for the holidays (see box, page 9). Many of the dishes can be eaten as a vegetarian main course as is or with the addition of a poached egg (such as Golden Flannel Hash, page 18, or Mixed-Mushroom Compotes, page 61), cheese, or tofu for protein. The salads, such as Crunchy Kale Slaw with Radishes (page 58), also make delicious choices for light, healthy lunches.

Shopping for Side Dishes

The first step to a great side dish is letting the market tell you when to make it. Whether you shop daily or on the weekends, go with what is in season and looks best that day. In other words, don't choose a recipe first, then force it to happen when the main ingredient looks past its prime. This book is organized as a handbook, so you can refer to it at the market or when you get home. Better to grab the corn or tomatoes at their absolute peak and make Creamed Corn with Chipotle and Queso Fresco (page 41) or Heirloom Tomato Panzanella with Burrata (page 86) than to head out with a must-have vegetable on your shopping list only to discover that its time has passed.

You will also find surefire seasonal recipes here that will allow you to plan ahead. Spring means asparagus, fava beans, and English peas, so consider recipes featuring those vegetables when your local markets start looking green. Fall is mushroom time, which means the compotes on page 61 are great then, but you can make them year-round with white mushrooms and shiitakes. Butternut squash is a standard for the holidays, but it stores well for months, making the Butternut Squash Puree with Brown Butter and Sage on page 90 a dish that can be served throughout the winter. Plus, some ingredients that you may think of as seasonal, like bell peppers, are available year-round, so you aren't tied to the calendar at all. And what about humble onions? They are so ubiquitous that we think of them only as a background ingredient, but make them star in a panade (page 62) and you'll have an amazing dish to fall back on any time of the year.

Whether or not you buy organic produce is a personal decision. Just bear in mind that organic growing methods are gentler on the environment, and that the produce they yield tends to taste better than its conventionally grown counterpart. Nowadays, some organic produce is cultivated in another hemisphere and flown long distances, however, so it may not be the wisest choice. And since organic food is not always accessible or affordable, the best advice is to shop locally and seasonally above all else.

A Matter of Taste (and Smell and Feel)

When you are choosing vegetables at the market, use all your senses to examine them. Check for vivid color and no rotten spots with your eyes, for the right texture and heft with your hands, for sunny fragrance (such as in tomatoes and herbs) with your nose, and even "scrunchiness" with your ears (a good indication that chard and other greens are really fresh). If you are lucky enough to encounter a vendor offering tastes, those bites are the perfect indicator if what is being sold is truly ripe.

At home, use all your senses when you cook, too. Often the most underrated is smell. We depend on our eyes and hands to guide us through the steps of a recipe, but it's our nose that will tell us when something is perfectly cooked. Just take a whiff of your kitchen when broccoli is roasting. At first it will smell raw, almost cabbagey, but when the exact moment of caramelization is reached, the fragrance will be sweet and toasty and irresistible. That's when it's time to open up the oven.

Then there's taste. The whole goal of this book is to get maximum flavor out of each of the forty ingredients. The choice of cooking method is crucial, but so is the balance of salt, fat, and acid in each recipe. Plus, there's the element of contrast. When the central ingredient is a vegetable or grain, the play of crunchy and soft, creamy and crisp, even hot and cold is what makes each recipe great. To achieve this, bread crumbs, nuts, cheese, spices, olives, fresh citrus and herbs, and preserved lemons are deployed in just the right combinations.

Cooking Side Dishes

You will find a lot of roasted vegetables in this book. The brassicas, such as cabbage, broccoli, and brussels sprouts, and the roots, like carrots and beets, benefit from the intense dry heat of an oven, which concentrates sugars and provides the sublime contrast of crunchy on the outside and soft and tender on the inside.

Other cooking methods used are sweating (letting the vegetable cook, covered, in its own juices), braising (covered, but with more liquid and other ingredients added to exchange flavors), sautéing or stir-frying (stirring quickly in an open pan with minimal fat), broiling (tucking dishes under the broiler to brown their surface), and grilling (cooking foods over an outdoor gas or charcoal grill). What you won't find is steaming, which drains away flavor rather than enhances it, or deep-frying, which masks an ingredient rather than highlights it.

To make cooking side dishes easy and efficient, you need just a few pieces of equipment. The most common is a sharp chef's knife. With it, you can prep almost everything in this book. For very fine slicing, a mandoline or a food processor is handy. Graters, including a box grater and a Microplane zester, are also practical.

A large, 10- to 12-inch (25- to 30-cm) sauté pan is indispensable. What distinguishes it from the relatively shallow, flare-sided frying pan (skillet) is its straight sides about 3 inches (7.5 cm) high and a snugly fitting cover. This single pan enables you to sauté, sweat, brown, braise, or sear, and the size is ideal for recipes serving four to six people. Round "all-purpose" pans with loop handles, stove-top woks, and wide frying pans also work, as long as they have a matching lid.

Because roasting is an essential method, you'll need a few sturdy baking sheets. Rimmed half sheet pans (18 by 13 by 1 inch/45 by 33 by 2.5 cm) are the best because the food won't roll off when you move the pan from counter to oven and back again. Parchment paper is crucial for roasting vegetables because it keeps the food from sticking, blots excess oil, and makes cleaning the baking sheet as simple as a wipe down.

THE SIDE DISHES PANTRY

Following are some essential ingredients you will need to create the recipes in this book.

BREAD CRUMBS Fine dried crumbs or Japanese panko (light, crystal-shaped crumbs) are ideal for crispy toppings. Or, if you have croutons on hand, put them in a plastic bag, then roll over the bag with a rolling pin to crush them into crumbs.

BROTH The term broth refers to store-bought, low-sodium broth, not homemade stock, although if you make your own stock, by all means use it. Most recipes call for vegetable broth or chicken broth, leaving the choice up to you. The only way to find a brand of broth that you like is to taste the different ones available.

BUTTER Use unsalted butter so that you can control the amount of salt added to a dish.

GARLIC This much-loved and fundamental kitchen staple adds great flavor to many recipes in this book. Look for plump heads with smooth, firm cloves and store whole garlic heads in a cool, dark place for up to 2 months.

OILS For cooking, an inexpensive, all-purpose olive oil is the most useful. When the taste of the oil makes a difference or for finishing a dish, such as a salad, the recipe will call for extra-virgin olive oil. When a neutral oil is preferred, grapeseed or canola will work.

ONIONS Nearly every supermarket offers onions in a variety of colors and sizes. Most recipes in which onions are used as a seasoning call for yellow onions. In the market, an average yellow onion weighs about 6 ounces (185 grams), which is the size that was used in creating these recipes.

PARMESAN If the specific flavor of imported Parmigiano-Reggiano makes a difference, that is what is called for in the ingredients list. If a less expensive version of Parmesan is fine, the recipe will call for Parmesan. To shred Parmesan (or other cheeses), use the large holes on a box grater; to grate it, use the small holes on a box grater, a Parmesan grater, or a Microplane grater. To shave Parmesan, use a swivel-bladed vegetable peeler or a cheese plane.

SALT Use flaky kosher salt for cooking for its clean flavor. Keep a ramekin or small bowl of it alongside the stove for cooking. It is easy to pinch up and blends in quickly. Use your own judgment and taste to determine how much salt is right. Sea salt, with its minerally flavor and crunchy texture, is sometimes listed for sprinkling over a finished dish.

BRAISED ARTICHOKES *with* MINT

1 lemon

12 small or 3 large artichokes, about 2 lb (1 kg) total weight

3 tbsp olive oil

1 leek, white part only, halved lengthwise, then thinly sliced crosswise

Salt

1 clove garlic, minced

½ cup (4 fl oz/125 ml) low-sodium vegetable or chicken broth or water

¼ cup (⅓ oz/10 g) roughly chopped fresh mint

Do as they do in Rome and use small artichokes in this dish, which don't have fuzzy centers. Sometimes labeled "baby" artichokes, they're actually the same age as the big ones; they just grow lower on the stalk, so they are smaller. If you can't find them, hearts of large artichokes can be used.

Finely grate the zest from the lemon and set the zest aside. Fill a large bowl with water, halve the lemon, and squeeze the juice into the water.

If using small artichokes, snap off the dark green outer leaves until you reach the tender yellow leaves. Using a small, sharp knife, trim away the tough, dark green outer layer of the base and the stem until the surface is smooth and evenly pale. Cut off the sharp tips of the leaves (about the top one-third), cut the artichoke in half lengthwise, and drop the halves into the lemon water to prevent discoloring.

If using large artichokes, cut the stem flush with the base. Snap off the dark green leaves until you reach the tender yellow leaves. Grasp the tops of the yellow leaves and pull them away to reveal the prickly, fuzzy choke. Using a spoon, scrape out and discard the choke. Using a small, sharp knife, trim the base as for the small artichokes. Quarter the heart and drop the quarters into the lemon water to prevent discoloring.

In a large sauté pan, warm the oil over medium-high heat. Add the leek and a good pinch of salt and sauté until very soft, about 4 minutes. Add the garlic and sauté for 30 seconds. Transfer the artichokes to the pan. Season with another pinch of salt, add the broth, and bring to a boil. Cover, reduce the heat to low, and simmer until the artichokes are tender when pierced with a knife, 18–20 minutes. Remove from the heat and stir in the mint and lemon zest. Transfer to a serving dish and serve warm or at room temperature.

SERVES 4

ARUGULA

Peppery arugula is so popular now that its sword-shaped leaves are available in a variety of sizes, from micro to macro. The best size for this dish is the "baby" arugula found in bins at the farmers' market.

ARUGULA SALAD *with* POMEGRANATES *and* PISTACHIOS

1 pomegranate	1 tbsp red wine vinegar
5 oz (155 g) small arugula leaves, rinsed and spun dry	Salt
½ cup (2 oz/60 g) pistachio meats	3 tbsp extra-virgin olive oil

Put a bowl in the sink. Cut the pomegranate in half horizontally (through the equator rather than through the stem end). Working over the bowl, put half of the pomegranate, cut side down, on the palm of your nondominant hand. Then, with your dominant hand, bang the back of a wooden spoon all over the skin side of the pomegranate half to release the seeds, which will fall between your fingers into the bowl. When you strike the pomegranate, be fairly forceful. At first the seeds will come out slowly, but they will soon start to fall out more quickly. Repeat with the second half of the pomegranate. Pick out any bits of white membrane from the bowl, then drain the seeds in a fine-mesh sieve and shake the sieve to release any excess moisture.

In a salad bowl, combine the arugula, pistachios, and pomegranate seeds. Drizzle with the vinegar and sprinkle with a good pinch of salt. Then drizzle with the oil and toss to mix evenly. Taste and correct with more vinegar and/or oil as desired. Serve right away.

SERVES 4

Asparagus *with* Hazelnut Gremolata

²/₃ cup (3 oz/90 g) hazelnuts

1 clove garlic, peeled

1 cup (1 oz/30 g) fresh flat-leaf parsley leaves

Grated zest of 1 organic orange

⅓ cup (3 fl oz/80 ml) extra-virgin olive oil, plus about 1 tsp

Salt

2 lb (1 kg) asparagus, tough ends trimmed

Trimming asparagus is a snap: just bend the cut end of each stalk and it will break naturally where the dry, tough end meets the moist upper stalk. If desired, use the ends to flavor broth for asparagus risotto or asparagus soup.

Preheat the oven to 375°F (190°C). Spread the nuts in a pie pan and toast in the oven, stirring once or twice, until the skins start to crack and the nuts are fragrant, about 12 minutes. Transfer the nuts to a fine-mesh sieve and put the sieve in the sink. Using a coarse-textured kitchen towel, rub the warm nuts against the sieve to slough off skins. Not every bit of skin will come off. Lift out the nuts and set aside.

To make the gremolata, turn on a food processor and drop the garlic through the feed tube to chop it. Turn off the processor, add the parsley, orange zest, and hazelnuts, and pulse until the nuts are finely chopped. Transfer to a small bowl, add the ⅓ cup oil and a pinch of salt, and stir to mix. Set aside for up to 1 hour to soften the sharp flavor of the raw garlic. Taste and adjust the seasoning with salt just before serving.

To cook the asparagus, position an oven rack about 4 inches (10 cm) from the heat element and preheat the broiler. Pile the asparagus on a rimmed baking sheet, drizzle evenly with the 1 tsp oil, sprinkle with a little salt, and then toss to coat the spears evenly. Spread the asparagus in a single layer on the baking sheet. Broil the spears, shaking the pan once or twice to turn them, until lightly charred and just tender, about 8 minutes.

Divide the asparagus among warmed individual plates and spoon a band of gremolata across each serving. Pass the remaining gremolata at the table.

SERVES 4

Golden beets can't be beat for this dish because they won't bleed color onto the potatoes the way red ones would. Although beets are in the market year-round, late summer and fall offer the best choice and flavor. Don't throw away the beet tops; they can be sautéed or cooked in soup just like Swiss chard (the two plants are cousins). The potatoes and beets can be roasted ahead of time and then cooled, covered, and refrigerated for up to 2 days before proceeding.

Golden Flannel Hash

1 lb (500 g) golden beets, trimmed, with ½ inch (12 mm) of stem intact

¾ lb (375 g) small Yukon gold potatoes

Salt and freshly ground pepper

2 tbsp olive oil

2 slices thick-cut bacon, chopped

1 small red onion, chopped

1 red bell pepper, seeded and chopped

1 tbsp unsalted butter

Chopped fresh flat-leaf parsley

Preheat the oven to 375°F (190°C). Enclose the beets in a large sheet of foil, crimping the foil closed. Place the packet on a rimmed baking sheet. Roast until a knife inserted into a beet through the foil slides in easily, 1–1½ hours, depending on the size of the beets. Remove from the oven and carefully open the foil. Let the beets stand until cool enough to handle, then peel and cut into ½-inch (12-mm) cubes.

In a saucepan, cover the potatoes with water by 2 inches (5 cm). Salt the water generously, bring to a boil over high heat, and cook until just tender when pierced with a knife, 12–15 minutes, depending on their size. Drain the potatoes and let stand until cool enough to handle, then peel and cut into ½-inch (12-mm) cubes.

In a large sauté pan, warm the oil over medium-high heat. Add the bacon, onion, and bell pepper and sauté until the vegetables are tender and the bacon fat is rendered, about 5 minutes. Add the butter, let it melt, and then add the potatoes, beets, and several grinds of pepper. Spread the vegetables in a single layer and cook, tamping down the vegetables with a spatula a few times to help develop a crust, until the potatoes begin to crisp on the bottom, about 10 minutes.

Divide the hash among warmed individual plates and sprinkle with parsley. Serve right away.

SERVES 4–6

BROCCOLI

Roasted Broccoli *with* Parmesan *and* Pepper Flakes

2 lb (1 kg) broccoli

3 tbsp olive oil

½ tsp red pepper flakes

Salt

1 tbsp fresh lemon juice

2-oz (60-g) chunk Parmigiano-Reggiano cheese

Preheat the oven to 375°F (190°C). Line a rimmed baking sheet with parchment paper.

Using a chef's knife, cut off the florets from each broccoli head, leaving about 1 inch (2.5 cm) of the stem attached. Set the large stems aside. Cut the florets into evenly sized pieces (see note). Cut off any leaves and discard. Now, trim off and discard the tough, fibrous bottom from each large stem, then remove the tough, woody outer skin by cutting off the 4 sides of the stem lengthwise. Cut each tender inner stem crosswise into 1-inch (2.5-cm) lengths.

Put all the broccoli pieces in a large serving bowl, drizzle with the oil, and sprinkle with the pepper flakes and a good pinch of salt. Toss to coat the broccoli evenly, then spread the broccoli in a single layer on a rimmed baking sheet (do not wash the bowl). Roast the broccoli, turning the pieces once with a spatula about halfway through the cooking time, until tender and just lightly charred, 25–30 minutes.

Remove the broccoli from the oven and return it to the bowl. Add the lemon juice and toss to distribute evenly. Using a vegetable peeler, shave shards of the cheese over the top. Serve right away.

SERVES 4

Think of this as nose-to-tail cooking for a vegetable: you put the whole head of broccoli to work. When cutting the florets, some will be small, some large, but you want them all about the same size. To cut the larger florets to match the smaller florets, slice them lengthwise through the stem to just above the base of the bud, then, using your fingers, pull the large floret apart into small, neat florets. Then cut up and use the stem, too.

*Broccoli rabe, raab,
rapini—the labeling of
this popular Italian
vegetable can be confusing,
but whatever it is called,
it should have medium-
thick green stalks, lots of
leaves, and small flower
buds. Slender, tree-like
broccolini is not the same
plant, but it can be cooked
this way, too.*

Spicy Broccoli Rabe *with* Anchovy *and* Preserved Lemon

Salt

1 bunch broccoli rabe, about
1 lb (500 g), tough ends trimmed
and stalks cut crosswise
into thirds

1 salt-packed anchovy, or 2 olive
oil–packed anchovy fillets

2 or 3 cloves garlic

¼ preserved lemon

3 tbsp olive oil

½ tsp Aleppo pepper flakes,
or ¼ tsp red pepper flakes

Bring a large pot of generously salted water to a boil. Drop in the
broccoli rabe, and when the water returns to a boil, cook for 1 minute.
Drain well and set aside. (At this point, the broccoli rabe can be
left standing at room temperature for up to 1 hour or covered and
refrigerated overnight.)

If using the salt-packed anchovy (which is preferred), rinse it under
cold running water, then gently pull each fillet away from the spine
and discard the spine and tail. On a cutting board, combine the
anchovy fillets, garlic to taste, and preserved lemon and mince
together with a chef's knife.

In a large sauté pan or wok, warm the oil over medium-high heat.
When hot, add the minced ingredients and the pepper flakes and
sauté until sizzling and fragrant, about 1 minute. Add the blanched
broccoli rabe and cook, tossing with tongs, until hot throughout
and well coated with the other ingredients, about 3 minutes. Transfer
to a warmed serving platter and serve right away.

SERVES 2–4

Roasted Brussels Sprouts *with* Bacon-Walnut Vinaigrette

1½ lb (750 g) brussels sprouts

2 tbsp olive oil

Salt and freshly ground pepper

3 slices thick-cut bacon, chopped

½ cup (2 oz/60 g) walnut halves, roughly chopped

2 tbsp maple syrup, preferably grade B

2 tbsp sherry vinegar

Like its cabbagey brethren broccoli and cauliflower, brussels sprouts taste much sweeter when roasted. Look for sprouts with bright green leaves that cling snugly to the little heads. As you trim each head, a few outer leaves will fall off. For an extra treat, toss the leaves with oil and salt and roast separately for 10 minutes to make crisp chips.

Preheat the oven to 425°F (220°C). Line a rimmed baking sheet with parchment paper.

Using a paring knife, trim off the base of each brussels sprout, then cut lengthwise into quarters. Place the sprout quarters in a bowl, add the oil and a good pinch of salt, and toss the sprouts with your hands until evenly coated. Spread the sprouts in an even layer on the prepared baking sheet and roast until tender and spotted with brown, about 25 minutes.

While the sprouts are cooking, in a nonstick frying pan, cook the bacon over medium heat, stirring as needed to prevent burning, until almost crisp, about 7 minutes. Stir in the walnuts and then the maple syrup and continue to sauté until the mixture is bubbly, about 2 minutes. Set the pan aside with the ingredients in it.

When the brussels sprouts are ready, transfer them to a serving bowl. Return the frying pan to medium-high heat, and when mixture starts to sizzle, stir in the vinegar and let cook until bubbly, about 10 seconds. Pour the bacon mixture over the sprouts, carefully scraping every bit from the pan into the bowl. Season with lots of pepper, then toss well and serve right away.

SERVES 4

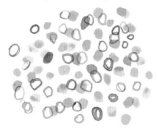

Bulgur, which is cracked and parboiled wheat with very little of the bran removed, is a whole grain, so it is extra good for you. Small, green Puy lentils, which originated in France and are now grown in North America, hold their shape better when cooked than brown lentils. Look for them in well-stocked markets.

BULGUR *and* LENTIL PILAF *with* TOASTED CASHEWS

½ cup (3½ oz/105 g) green lentils, preferably Puy

Boiling water to cover

2 tbsp olive oil

1 small yellow onion, chopped

Salt

⅔ cup (3½ oz/105 g) raw cashews

1 tsp ground coriander

1 cup (6 oz/185 g) bulgur

3 oz (90 g) feta cheese, crumbled (optional)

Thinly sliced tender green onion tops for garnish

Pick through the lentils and discard any small stones or debris. Put the lentils in a heatproof bowl and add boiling water to cover by 1 inch (2.5 cm). Cover the bowl with a flat plate or with foil and let stand for 15 minutes.

Meanwhile, in a large sauté pan, warm the oil over high heat. Add the onion, sprinkle with a pinch of salt, and sauté until the onion is coated with the oil and starts to soften, about 1 minute. Reduce the heat to medium and cook, stirring occasionally, until pale gold, about 5 minutes. Add the cashews and coriander and sauté until the cashews are lightly toasted, about 5 minutes longer.

Add the bulgur to the pan and stir until coated with the oil and onion, about 1 minute. Drain the lentils, add to the pan, and then stir in 3 cups (24 fl oz/750 ml) water and 1 tsp salt. Let the mixture come to a boil, then reduce the heat to medium-low, cover, and simmer until the bulgur and lentils are cooked through, about 15 minutes.

Uncover the pan and rake the mixture with a fork to fluff it. Divide among individual plates and top each portion with feta, if desired. Garnish with the green onions and serve right away.

SERVES 4–6

Warm Red Cabbage Salad *with* Goat Cheese

½ cup (2 oz/60 g) walnuts

2 tbsp olive oil

5 cups (15 oz/470 g) shredded red cabbage (about ½ large or ¾ medium head)

Salt and freshly ground pepper

3 tbsp red wine vinegar

2 tbsp walnut oil or more olive oil

2 oz (60 g) fresh goat cheese, crumbled

Snipped fresh chives for garnish

Preheat the oven to 375°F (190°C). Spread the walnuts in a pie pan and toast in the oven, stirring once or twice, until fragrant, about 10 minutes. Remove the nuts from the oven. If the nuts have skins, wrap them in a coarse-textured kitchen towel, and rub them vigorously with the towel to slough off some of the skins (it's okay if the nuts break up into smaller pieces as you do this). Not every bit of skin will come off. Lift the nuts from the towel, leaving the skins behind. Chop the nuts roughly and set aside.

In a large sauté pan, warm the olive oil over medium-high heat. Add the cabbage and a generous pinch of salt, stir well, and cover the pan. Let the cabbage sweat for about 2 minutes to draw out the moisture. Uncover and sauté until the cabbage is limp and starts to darken, about 5 minutes. Stir in the vinegar and cook for 2 minutes longer (the color will brighten again).

Remove from the heat and stir in the walnut oil and walnuts, then season with salt and lots of pepper. Divide the cabbage among warmed individual plates and top each portion with a scattering of goat cheese and chives. Serve right away.

SERVES 4

Sturdy red cabbage stands up well to sautéing and looks more vivid on the plate than the green variety. To shred it, cut the head into quarters, slice away the core, then cut crosswise with a chef's knife. Or, to speed up the task, use a food processor fitted with the shredding disk. Be sure to toast and then rub the walnuts to remove some of the astringent skin.

CARROTS

What's up with carrots, Doc? You can find orange ones, purple ones, baby ones and big ones, and even mini ones that are actually shaved-down large carrots. Use any of them for this dish, except the flavorless minis. If using true baby carrots, roast them whole.

Sweet-Hot Roasted Carrots

2½ lb (1.25 kg) carrots, peeled and cut into sticks 3 inches (7.5 cm) long and ½ inch (12 mm) wide and thick

1 tbsp olive oil

½ tsp salt

1 lime

2 tbsp honey

⅛ tsp cayenne pepper, or to taste

Position 2 racks in the center of the oven. Preheat the oven to 400°F (200°C). Line 2 rimmed baking sheets with parchment paper.

In a large bowl, combine the carrots, oil, and salt and toss to coat the carrots evenly. Put half of the carrots on each prepared baking sheet, spreading them out in a single layer. Roast the carrots, turning them with tongs halfway through the cooking time, until lightly caramelized in spots, about 35 minutes.

Meanwhile, grate the zest from the lime, then halve the lime and squeeze enough juice to total about 1½ tbsp. About 5 minutes before the carrots are done, in a very small pan, combine the honey, lime zest and juice, and cayenne pepper over medium heat and stir until hot and bubbly.

When the carrots are ready, remove from the oven, pour the honey mixture evenly over them, and turn them with tongs to coat well. Taste a carrot and add more lime juice, cayenne, and/or salt as desired. Transfer to a warmed serving dish and serve right away.

SERVES 4

If you can find an orange cauliflower (check your local farmers' market), the electric hue is a fun way to amp up the curried color of this dish, although a classic white one is fine. Don't amp up the amount of curry, however, or that's all you will taste.

CURRIED ROASTED CAULIFLOWER

1 large head cauliflower, about 1¼ lb (625 g)

3 tbsp olive oil

1 tsp Madras curry powder

¾ tsp salt

Preheat the oven to 400°F (200°C). Line a rimmed baking sheet with parchment paper.

Using a paring knife, cut away the leaves and the core from the cauliflower. Break or slice the cauliflower into evenly sized florets 2–3 inches (5–7.5 cm) long, without cutting off too much of the stems.

In a large bowl, combine the oil, curry powder, and salt and stir to mix well. Add the cauliflower and toss to coat evenly. Spread the florets in a single layer on the prepared baking sheet.

Roast the florets until just tender and tinged with brown around the edges, about 35 minutes. Transfer to a serving dish and serve right away.

SERVES 4

Why is celery usually relegated to the stock pot when its flavor and texture can add so much to a dish? Use the dark green outer ribs of the celery head, as they have more crunch and a saltier taste than the pale inner ribs. You can use day-old or even older bread; if it has become too hard to tear, soften for 30 seconds in the microwave. If you want to make this dish ahead, after mixing the ingredients together in the bowl, cover and refrigerate for up to 4 hours before baking.

CELERY *and* APPLE STUFFING

½ cup (4 oz/125 g) unsalted butter, plus more for the baking dish

1 lb (500 g) stale coarse country white bread or focaccia, torn into 1-inch (2.5-cm) chunks

5 outer celery ribs, cut lengthwise into thirds, then diced crosswise

1 small yellow onion, chopped

1 large Golden Delicious or Granny Smith apple, about ½ lb (250 g), halved, cored, and diced

1 cup (4 oz/125 g) jarred peeled chestnuts, chopped

¼ cup (⅓ oz/10 g) finely chopped fresh flat-leaf parsley leaves

2 tbsp minced fresh sage

1 tbsp *each* minced fresh rosemary and thyme

About 3 cups (24 fl oz/750 ml) low-sodium vegetable or chicken broth

Salt

Preheat the oven to 350°F (180°C). Butter the bottom and sides of a 9-by-13-inch (23-by-33-cm) or 3-qt (3-l) baking dish.

Put the bread in a very large bowl and set aside. In a large sauté pan, melt the butter over medium-high heat. Add the celery and onion and sauté until they start to soften, about 2 minutes. Transfer the contents of the pan to the bowl with the bread, then add the apple, chestnuts, and herbs to the bowl.

In a saucepan, warm 2½ cups (20 fl oz/625 ml) of the broth over medium heat until just steaming (or heat the broth in a large glass measuring cup in a microwave). Pour the hot broth over the bread mixture and, using a large spoon, toss until the bread is evenly and thoroughly moistened. If it seems dry, add up to ½ cup (4 fl oz/125 ml) more broth. Season with salt, then spread in the prepared dish.

Cover with foil and bake for 30 minutes. Uncover and bake until lightly toasted on top, about 25 minutes longer. Serve right away.

SERVES 8–10

CELERY ROOT RÉMOULADE

¹⁄₃ cup (3 fl oz/80 ml) mayonnaise

¹⁄₄ cup (2 fl oz/60 ml) fresh
lemon juice

1 tbsp caper brine

1 tsp Dijon mustard

1 large celery root,
about 1¹⁄₄ lb (625 g)

2–3 tsp chopped fresh tarragon

Salt

To make the dressing, in a small bowl, whisk together the mayonnaise, lemon juice, caper brine, and mustard until well blended. Set aside.

Place the celery root on a cutting board and cut a slice off each end to expose the flesh. Stand the celery root on one flat end and slice off the peel all the way around, cutting from the top to the bottom. Trim away any brown spots. Cut the celery root in half, then cut lengthwise into wedges just thick enough to fit a food processor feed tube. Fit a food processor with the shredding disk, or fit a mandoline with the julienne blade, and coarsely shred the wedges. (Do not use a box grater, which will yield a mushy result.) Put the shredded celery root in a large serving bowl.

Immediately pour the dressing over the celery root and toss well with a spoon and fork as you would a salad. Add the tarragon 1 tsp at a time, tasting until you get the flavor you like. Season with salt and serve, or cover and refrigerate for up to 1 hour before serving.

SERVES 4–6

Available from autumn through early spring, celery root (aka celeriac) has a tough-looking exterior. To get at the tender, mild, ivory flesh under the gnarly brown carapace, trim the root as you would a pineapple. The magic factor in this preparation is the salty caper brine; use the capers themselves in the pan-grilled radicchio recipe on page 70.

CHARD

Pick a chard, any chard:
green, red, or rainbow all
work in this recipe. Look
for leaves that aren't too
"leggy"; in other words,
you want a high ratio of
leaf to stem because the
stems are not used here.
The chard stems can
be used to add extra
nutrients and texture to
a minestrone or gratin.

Swiss Chard *with* Currants *and* Pine Nuts

⅓ cup (2 oz/60 g) dried currants	2 tbsp pine nuts
2 tbsp sherry vinegar	3 tbsp olive oil
Salt	1 shallot, thinly sliced
2 bunches Swiss chard, about 1½ lb (750 g) total weight	

In a small bowl, combine the currants and vinegar. Add a pinch of salt and hot water to cover; then set aside to plump. Working with 1 chard leaf at time, lay it on a cutting board and, using a sharp knife, cut along both sides of the stem to remove the leaf in 2 pieces; reserve the stems for another use. Stack the leaves and, using a chef's knife, cut them crosswise into thick strips. Rinse well in a colander.

Pour water to a depth of 2 inches (5 cm) into a large pot and add a good pinch of salt. Bring to a boil over high heat, then add the chard. Cover and cook until the chard is just tender and no longer tastes raw, 4–5 minutes. Drain well in a colander and set aside.

In a dry large sauté pan, toast the pine nuts over medium heat, shaking the pan often, until they are golden and smell toasty, about 2 minutes. Pour onto a plate to cool. Add the oil to the same pan and return to medium heat. When the oil is hot, add the shallot and sauté until soft and golden, 3–5 minutes. Add the drained chard and stir until well coated with the oil. Cover the pan, reduce the heat to medium-low, and cook until the chard is very tender, about 5 minutes.

Drain the currants, stir them into the chard, and remove from the heat. Let stand for a minute or two, then season the chard with salt. Transfer to a warmed platter or divide among individual plates. Scatter the pine nuts over the top and serve right away.

SERVES 4

CREAMED CORN *with* CHIPOTLE *and* QUESO FRESCO

5 ears white or yellow corn, husks and silk removed, or 4 cups (1½ lb/750 g) frozen corn kernels, unthawed

2 tbsp unsalted butter

Salt

²/₃ cup (5 fl oz/160 ml) heavy cream

1 chipotle chile in adobo sauce, including the sauce clinging to it, minced

1 lime, halved

About 3 tbsp crumbled queso fresco

To get the creamiest corn, you need to "milk" the cobs, which means you must scrape the emptied-out kernel pockets with a knife to extract every drop of sweet, milky liquid left behind. If you are craving this dish after corn season has passed, frozen corn can be substituted.

If using ears of corn, working with 1 ear at a time, hold it upright, stem end down, in a wide, flat bowl, and, using a chef's knife, cut straight down between the kernels and the cob, being careful to avoid the fibrous bases of the kernels and rotating the ear after each cut. When all of the kernels have been cut off, run the spine of the knife down the length of the cob to extract all of the "milk" from the base of the kernels.

In a large sauté pan, melt the butter over medium-high heat. Add the fresh or frozen corn kernels and a good pinch of salt and stir for 1 minute to heat through. Reduce the heat to medium-low, cover, and let the corn sweat in its own juices until just tender, about 8 minutes. Stir in the cream and chile and bring the mixture a boil. Reduce the heat to medium-low and cook, stirring often, until the cream is thick and mostly absorbed by the corn, about 5 minutes.

Squeeze the juice from ½ lime into the pan, stir well, then taste and add more lime juice and salt as needed to balance the sweetness of the corn. Divide among warmed individual plates and top with the queso fresco. Serve right away.

SERVES 4

COUSCOUS

The trick to preventing lumps from forming when preparing couscous, the pasta of North Africa, is to toast the grains in oil before adding the liquid, and then to fluff up the cooked grains with a fork just before serving.

Spiced Couscous

1 tsp ground cumin

1 tsp ground coriander

1/2 tsp ground ginger

Salt

2 tbsp olive oil

1 1/2 cups (9 oz/280 g) instant couscous

1/2 cup (3 oz/90 g) golden raisins

2 1/2 cups (20 fl oz/625 ml) boiling water

In a small bowl, stir together the cumin, coriander, ginger, and 1 tsp salt. In a saucepan, warm the oil over medium-high heat. When hot, stir in the spice-salt mixture and sauté for 10 seconds.

Add the couscous and raisins to the pan and sauté for 1 minute to toast the couscous. Pour in the boiling water; the mixture will bubble vigorously. When the bubbles calm down, stir the couscous once, then cover the pan, remove from the heat, and let sit for 7 minutes.

Uncover and rake the couscous with a fork to fluff the grains and eliminate any lumps. Mound the couscous in a warmed serving dish or divide among warmed individual plates and serve right away.

SERVES 4

Braised Moroccan Eggplant

1 large Italian eggplant, about 1 lb (500 g), trimmed and cut into ½-inch (12-mm) cubes

Salt

1 tsp *each* ground cumin and sweet paprika

½ tsp ground coriander

1 can (14 oz/440 g) whole plum tomatoes, with juice

¼ cup (2 fl oz/60 ml) extra-virgin olive oil

2 cloves garlic, smashed

½ cup (¾ oz/20 g) *each* chopped fresh mint and cilantro

2 tbsp minced preserved lemon peel (optional)

Put the eggplant cubes in a colander, sprinkle with 1 tsp salt, and toss to coat evenly. Set the colander in a sink and let the eggplant stand for 10 minutes (liquid will bead up on the flesh). Meanwhile, in a small bowl, stir together the cumin, paprika, and coriander. Pour the tomatoes and their juice into a bowl and crush the tomatoes with your hand or a potato masher.

In a large sauté pan or wok, warm the oil and garlic over medium-high heat, swirling the pan to flavor the oil with the garlic, until the garlic starts to sizzle but does not color, about 1 minute. Add the eggplant (do not rinse off salt) and stir until well coated with the oil. Pour in ¼ cup (2 fl oz/60 ml) water and bring it to a boil. Cover, reduce heat to medium-low, and cook until the eggplant is tender, about 10 minutes. Uncover and gently stir in the tomatoes. Raise the heat to medium-high and let cook, uncovered, at a brisk simmer, shaking the pan occasionally, until the tomatoes thicken, about 10 minutes longer.

Remove from the heat, gently stir in the mint and cilantro, and remove and discard the garlic, if desired. Transfer the eggplant to a serving dish, sprinkle with the preserved lemon, if using, and serve warm or at room temperature.

SERVES 4

Similar though smaller than the American globe eggplant, the Italian variety is deep purple, oblong, and wider at the blossom end than the stem end. In the past, cooks salted cut raw eggplant to reduce the bitterness, but that quality has been bred out. Nowadays, salting is a good way to keep this versatile vegetable from absorbing too much oil.

Elegant, pale Belgian endives—they grow without light so they will not deepen in color—look particularly chic belted with prosciutto. Make sure to purchase firm, snugly furled heads with just a touch of light yellow on the leaf tips. To prep endive, remove any discolored outer leaves and then trim the base just enough to cut away any brown spots.

ROASTED ENDIVE *with* PROSCIUTTO

4 heads Belgian endive, trimmed

8 paper-thin slices prosciutto

3 tbsp olive oil, or as needed

½ cup (4 fl oz/125 ml) low-sodium vegetable or chicken broth

1 tbsp unsalted butter

¼ cup (1 oz/30 g) shredded Asiago or Parmesan cheese

Freshly ground black pepper

Minced fresh flat-leaf Italian parsley leaves, for garnish

Preheat the oven to 400°F (200°C). Halve the endives lengthwise. Wrap each half endive around the middle with a slice of prosciutto to "belt" it. If the prosciutto slice is too short, cut it in half lengthwise and wrap the pieces end to end. Select a baking dish just large enough to accommodate the endive halves in a snug single layer and reserve.

In a large sauté pan, warm the oil over medium-high heat until it ripples. Lay the endives, cut side down, in a single layer in the pan (if they don't all fit, brown them in batches, adding more oil as needed) and cook until slightly browned on the cut sides, about 1½ minutes. Using tongs, turn the endives over and brown lightly on the second side, about 1 minute longer. Transfer the endives to the baking dish.

Pour the broth into the sauté pan and scrape up any browned bits on the pan bottom. Swirl in the butter until it melts, then pour the mixture over and around the endives in the baking dish. Sprinkle the cheese evenly over the top. Roast until the endives are tender when pierced with a knife and the cheese is browned and crusty, 30–35 minutes.

Remove the endives from the oven, grind pepper over the top, and transfer them to a warmed platter or individual plates. Spoon the cooking juices over the endives, sprinkle with parsley, and serve.

SERVES 4

ENGLISH PEA *and* ONION GRATIN

2 tbsp unsalted butter, at room
temperature, plus more for the dish

⅓ cup (½ oz/15 g) panko

⅓ cup (1½ oz/45 g) freshly grated
Parmesan cheese

1 lb (500 g) fresh or frozen
pearl onions

2 cups (10 oz/315 g) fresh or thawed
frozen English peas

¾ cup (6 fl oz/180 ml) low-sodium
vegetable or chicken broth

½ cup (4 fl oz/125 ml) heavy cream

1 tbsp all-purpose flour

Preheat the oven to 450°F (230°C). Butter the bottom and sides of
a 10-inch (25-cm) gratin dish or other 1½-qt (1.5 l) baking dish.

In a bowl, stir together the panko and cheese. Set aside. If using
fresh pearl onions, prepare an ice-water bath. Drop the onions into
a saucepan of boiling water and cook for 1 minute. Drain, then
transfer to the ice water to stop the cooking. When the onions are
cool enough to handle, use a paring knife to cut off the stem end
and peel away the skin. Trim off any long roots, but keep the root
end intact. If using frozen pearl onions, rinse them in a colander.

In a saucepan, melt 1 tbsp of the butter over medium-high heat.
If using fresh peas, add them along with the onions. Pour in the
broth and cream, bring to a boil, and cook until the vegetables are
just tender and the liquid is reduced, about 5 minutes. If using
frozen peas, stir them in at the end of the 5 minutes.

In a small bowl, using a wooden spoon, mash together the remaining
1 tbsp butter and the flour to make a thick paste. Stir this into the
pan with the peas and onions and cook for 1 minute more. Pour the
mixture into the prepared dish and sprinkle the panko mixture evenly
over the top. Bake until the topping is golden and the mixture is
bubbly, about 12 minutes. Let stand for 5–10 minutes before serving.

SERVES 4

*Pease, please. That's
the old English spelling
for beloved garden peas,
and this is a particularly
British way to serve them.
To make quick work of
shelling peas, snap off the
stem end, pull the string
along the length of the
pod, then use your thumb
to pop open the pod and
free the peas. If you are
using fresh peas, plan on
about 2 lb (1kg) in the
pod before shelling.*

It's no longer hard to find farro in grocery stores, but look for packages that say semiperlato, or semi-pearled, which means that some of the bran layer has been removed, so the grain cooks more quickly. You can use any winter squash for this, but buying precut butternut squash saves time in the kitchen.

FARRO *with* WINTER SQUASH *and* PECANS

1 cup (6 oz/185 g) semiperlato farro

2 tbsp unsalted butter

1 tbsp olive oil

½ yellow onion, finely chopped

Salt

2½ cups (20 fl oz/625 ml) low-sodium vegetable or chicken broth

2 cups (about 8 oz/250 g) winter squash cubes (½-inch/12-mm cubes)

½ cup (2 oz/60 g) pecans halves, coarsely chopped

1 tsp finely chopped fresh rosemary

Put the farro in a fine-mesh sieve, rinse under cold running water, and shake dry thoroughly.

In a large sauté pan, melt 1 tbsp of the butter with the oil over medium-high heat. Add the onion and a generous pinch of salt and sauté until tender, about 5 minutes. Add the farro and stir for about 1 minute to coat with the fat. Pour in 1½ cups (12 fl oz/375 ml) of the broth and let come to a boil. Reduce the heat to medium-low heat, cover, and simmer for 15 minutes.

Uncover and stir in the squash and the remaining 1 cup (8 fl oz/ 250 ml) broth. Raise the heat to high and bring to a boil, stirring, then reduce the heat to medium-low, cover, and simmer until the squash is tender and the grains are tender but still chewy, 15–20 minutes longer. If any broth remains in the pan, cook, uncovered, until it is absorbed.

While the farro is cooking, melt the remaining 1 tbsp butter in a small frying pan over medium heat. Add the pecans, rosemary, and a pinch of salt and sauté until the nuts smell toasty, about 1½ minutes. Set aside.

When the farro is ready, transfer to a warmed serving dish, top with the nuts, and serve right away.

SERVES 4

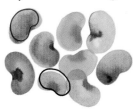

*Nothing says spring
like a green, green fava
bean. For this dish, look
for larger beans that
have some heft to them.
Because shelling the
beans and then peeling
each one can take time,
use it as an excuse to
gather a few friends
to share the work.*

Fava Bean *and* Celery Salad *with* Ricotta Salata

1½ lb (750 g) fava beans, shelled

4 outer celery ribs, thinly sliced on the diagonal

3 tbsp extra-virgin olive oil

Grated zest of 1 lemon

1 tbsp fresh lemon juice

Salt and freshly ground pepper

2-oz (60-g) chunk ricotta salata, pecorino, or Parmigiano-Reggiano cheese

Bring a saucepan filled with water to a boil. Drop the shelled fava beans into the boiling water and cook for 3 minutes. Drain and let the favas cool slightly, then slit the skin with a paring knife and pop out the inner bean. Discard the skins and place the favas in a bowl.

Add the celery, oil, and lemon zest and juice to the favas, season with salt and pepper, and toss to mix well. Divide the mixture among individual plates and, using a vegetable peeler, shave the cheese over the top. Serve right away.

SERVES 4

Fennel is a member of the parsley family, so it's no wonder its feathery tops make such a good garnish. Look for fennel bulbs with the stalks and fronds still attached and save the fronds for sprinkling over the finished dish. Keeping the core attached when cutting the fennel into wedges helps it hold together as it cooks.

CARAMELIZED FENNEL
with SHALLOTS *and* OLIVES

3 large fennel bulbs with fronds, stalks removed and fronds reserved

4 shallots

1 tsp minced fresh rosemary

Salt

3 tbsp olive oil

¼ cup (1½ oz/45 g) dry-cured or Niçoise olives, pitted

1 tbsp balsamic vinegar

Preheat the oven to 400°F (200°C). Line a rimmed baking sheet with parchment paper.

Trim the base of each fennel bulb just enough to remove any brown spots, then discard the outer bulb layer if tough or discolored. Cut each bulb in half lengthwise, then cut each half into 6 wedges, keeping the cores attached. Put the wedges in a large bowl.

Trim off the top and root end of each shallot, then peel the shallot to reveal the 2 lobes. Cut each lobe in half lengthwise (if there is only 1 lobe, cut it in half). Add the shallots to the bowl holding the fennel. Add the rosemary, a generous pinch of salt, and the oil and toss to coat evenly.

Spread the vegetables in a single layer on the prepared baking sheet. Roast the fennel and shallots, turning them once halfway through the cooking time, until tender and starting to caramelize, about 40 minutes.

When the vegetables are ready, remove from the oven, scatter the olives over the top, drizzle evenly with the vinegar, and toss lightly with the spatula. Return to the oven for 5 more minutes.

Transfer to a serving platter and garnish with the fennel fronds, if using. Serve right away.

SERVES 4

If you've eaten only squeaky-to-the-bite, barely cooked green beans, you will be amazed what a difference slow cooking makes. When shopping, select beans with firm, crisp pods with even color and no bumpy hints of the beans inside.

SLOW-COOKED GREEK-STYLE GREEN BEANS

¼ cup (2 fl oz/60 ml) extra-virgin olive oil

3 cloves garlic, thinly sliced

1 lb (500 g) green beans, stem ends trimmed and cut into 2-inch (5-cm) lengths

Pinch of red pepper flakes

Salt

2 ripe tomatoes, about 1 lb (500 g) total weight, halved, seeded, and chopped, or 1 cup (8 oz/250 g) drained canned tomatoes, chopped

2 tsp chopped fresh dill

¼ cup (1¼ oz/35 g) crumbled feta cheese (optional)

In a large sauté pan or wok, warm the oil and garlic over medium-high heat, swirling the pan to flavor the oil with the garlic, until the garlic starts to sizzle but does not color, about 1 minute. Add the green beans, pepper flakes, and a generous pinch of salt and stir to coat the beans well with the oil and seasonings. Add the tomatoes, raise the heat to high, and bring the mixture to a boil. Reduce the heat to low, cover, and cook until the beans are very tender and almost khaki colored, about 40 minutes.

Uncover and stir in the dill. Transfer the mixture to a warmed serving bowl, sprinkle the feta over the top, if using, and serve right away.

SERVES 4

There was a time when curly kale was considered alternative-lifestyle, hippie food. Then came smooth, dark, suave Tuscan kale and heads turned. Markets label it in a variety of ways, including dinosaur, Lacinato, and cavolo nero. To get the slaw effect, you must shred, not tear, the leaves. To prep kale, working with 1 kale leaf at a time, lay it on a cutting board and, using a sharp knife, cut along both sides of the stem to remove the leaf in 2 pieces. Discard the stems.

CRUNCHY KALE SLAW *with* RADISHES

¾ lb (375 g) Tuscan kale, stems removed (see note)

6 large red radishes, tops trimmed

1 green onion, white and tender green parts, thinly sliced

2 tbsp cider vinegar

1 tsp Dijon mustard

Salt

3 tbsp extra-virgin olive oil

2 tbsp plus ½ tsp canola or grapeseed oil

¼ cup (1 oz/30 g) raw pumpkin or sunflower seeds

½ cup (2½ oz/75 g) crumbled cotija or feta cheese

Preheat the oven to 400°F (200°C).

Stack the kale leaves and shred them crosswise into thin strips. Rinse well in a colander, spin dry, and put into a large salad bowl. Cut each radish in half. Place each half, cut side down, and slice thinly. Stack the slices and cut into a fine julienne. Add the radishes and green onions to the kale.

In a small bowl, using a fork, whisk together the vinegar, mustard, and a pinch of salt until blended. Drizzle in the olive oil and the 2 tbsp canola oil while whisking constantly until emulsified. Pour the vinaigrette evenly over the vegetables in the salad bowl and set aside while you toast the pumpkin seeds.

Put the seeds in a small bowl, add the ½ tsp canola oil and a pinch of salt, and toss well. Spread the seeds in a pie pan and toast in the oven, stirring once, until lightly browned, about 7 minutes.

Add the toasted seeds and the cheese to the slaw, toss well, and serve right away.

SERVES 4–6

MIXED-MUSHROOM COMPOTES

2 tbsp unsalted butter

1 shallot, minced

½ lb (250 g) white or cremini mushrooms, cleaned (see note) and thinly sliced

¼ lb (125 g) fresh shiitake or other exotic mushrooms, cleaned (see note) and thinly sliced

Salt and freshly ground pepper

¼ cup (2 fl oz/60 ml) Marsala or sherry

¾ cup (6 fl oz/180 ml) heavy cream

1½ tsp soy sauce

1 tsp fresh thyme leaves, or ¼ tsp dried thyme

¼ cup (1 oz/30 g) freshly grated Parmesan cheese

¼ cup (½ oz/15 g) crushed crispy croutons or panko

In a large sauté pan, melt the butter over medium heat. Add the shallot and sauté until soft and fragrant, about 1 minute. Stir in the mushrooms and a generous pinch of salt, then cover and sweat the mushrooms until they soften and release their liquid, 3–5 minutes. Uncover, pour in the Marsala, bring to a boil, and boil for 30 seconds. Stir in the cream, soy sauce, and thyme and let the mixture return to a boil and thicken just slightly (you don't want the cream to be completely absorbed). Remove from heat and season with pepper.

Divide the mushroom mixture evenly among four ½-cup (4-fl oz/ 125-ml) flame-proof ramekins. (The compotes can be made ahead to this point and set aside for up to 1 hour. To serve, place them in a preheated 400°F/200°C oven until bubbly, about 10 minutes, then proceed as directed next.) Preheat the broiler and position a rack about 4 inches (10 cm) from the heat element. Arrange the ramekins on a rimmed baking sheet. In a small bowl, stir together the Parmesan and croutons and sprinkle over the ramekins. Broil until golden brown on top, 1–2 minutes. Serve right away.

SERVES 4

Mushrooms aren't as wild as you may think. Most exotic varieties, from oyster and shiitake to king trumpet and maitake, are cultivated; rare (and expensive) are the foraged varieties, such as morel, chanterelle, and porcini. Use any blend of mushrooms for this recipe; a mix of cremini and shiitake tastes a lot like truffles. To clean mushrooms, wipe the caps clean with a damp towel (check the gills of exotic mushrooms carefully for dirt), then trim off the tough stem ends (if using shiitakes, remove the entire stem).

Members of the onion clan often play secondary roles, but the assertive yellow onion and the mild leek are center stage in these savory bread puddings (minus the eggs). When working with leeks, be extra-sure that you clean them well to remove the grit that naturally settles inside the layers. This is a great way to recycle leftover crusty bread. Half of a 1-lb (500-g) loaf, with the crusts sliced off, will be the right amount.

ONION *and* LEEK PANADES

3 tbsp unsalted butter, plus more for the ramekins

1 large leek, about ¾ lb (375 g), root and dark green top removed

1 lb (500 g) yellow onions, chopped

Salt and freshly ground pepper

½ cup (4 fl oz/125 ml) dry white wine

6 oz (185 g) crustless day-old bread, cut into small cubes

½ cup (4 fl oz/125 ml) *each* heavy cream and low-sodium vegetable or chicken broth

1 cup (4 oz/125 g) shredded Gruyère cheese

¼ tsp freshly grated nutmeg

Butter six ¾-cup (6–fl oz/180-ml) ramekins or other individual baking dishes. Place the dishes on a rimmed baking sheet.

Cut the leek in half lengthwise, then thinly slice crosswise. Put the slices in a bowl generously filled with cold water and swish with your hand to release any grit. Set the bowl next to the stove. In a large sauté pan, melt the 3 tbsp butter over medium-high heat. Add the onions and 1 tsp salt and sauté until soft, about 4 minutes. Using a slotted spoon, transfer the leeks from the water to the pan, then reduce the heat to medium and cook, stirring often, until the onions and leek are very soft, about 12 minutes. Pour in the wine and cook for 1 minute. Remove from the heat.

Preheat the oven to 375°F (190°C). Place the bread cubes in a large bowl and add the onion-leek mixture, cream, broth, ⅔ cup (2½ oz/80 g) of the cheese, the nutmeg, and a few grinds of pepper. Stir well, then let stand for 10 minutes.

Divide the bread mixture evenly among the prepared ramekins. Sprinkle the with the remaining ⅓ cup (1½ oz/45 g) cheese. Bake until the tops are crusty and the panades are warmed through, about 30 minutes. Let cool for about 5 minutes before serving.

SERVES 6

Parnsip *and* Carrot Latkes

PARSNIPS

½ lb (250 g) parsnips, peeled

½ lb (250 g) carrots, peeled

1 lb (500 g) russet potatoes, peeled

2 tbsp minced shallot

¼ cup (1½ oz/45 g) all-purpose flour

1 tsp baking powder

Salt

2 large eggs, beaten

Grapeseed or canola oil for frying

Sour cream, for serving (optional)

Preheat the oven to 300°F (150°C). Line 2 rimmed baking sheets with parchment paper.

One at a time, using the coarse holes of a box grater, grate the parsnips, carrots, and potatoes. Transfer to a bowl, add the shallot, and mix well. Add the flour, baking powder, and 1 tsp salt and toss with your hands to mix thoroughly. Add the eggs and stir with a fork until well blended.

In a wide frying pan, heat 3 tbsp oil over medium-high heat. Fry a test nugget of the vegetable mixture until golden brown, taste, and add more salt to the remaining mixture if needed. Then, working in batches to prevent crowding, scoop up about 1 tbsp of the vegetable mixture for each latke, gently drop it into the hot pan, and pat down slightly to flatten. Cook, turning once, until golden brown on both sides, about 5 minutes total. Using a slotted spatula, transfer to a prepared baking sheet and place in the oven to keep warm until ready to serve. Cook the remaining vegetable mixture the same way, adding more oil to the pan as needed to prevent sticking.

Arrange the latkes on a warmed platter with a small bowl of sour cream alongside, if using. Serve right away.

SERVES 6–8

Because parsnips are sweet-tasting roots, they go together deliciously with carrots. Choose good-sized specimens or they will be awkward to grate. And don't be tempted to save time by using a food processor for the grating step, as too much water will be released and the latkes won't crisp properly.

*You will need about
2 lb (1 kg) of mixed
peppers for this recipe.
If you cannot find a
variety of colors, you
can use all one color.
Just be sure not use
only green bell peppers,
however, as they are
not fully ripe and
thus not sweet enough
on their own.*

SWEET *and* HOT PEPERONATA

1 red bell pepper	**2 large cloves garlic, smashed**
1 orange bell pepper	**1 bay leaf**
1 yellow bell pepper	**Salt**
1 poblano chile	**3 tbsp red wine vinegar**
¼ cup (2 fl oz/60 ml) olive oil	**1 tbsp sugar**

Cut all of the bell peppers into quarters lengthwise and discard
the stems, seeds, and ribs. Slice each quarter lengthwise into strips
¼ inch (6 mm) wide. Cut the poblano chile in half lengthwise
and discard the stem, seeds, and ribs. Slice each half crosswise into
strips ¼ inch (6 mm) wide.

In a large sauté pan or skillet, warm the oil and garlic over medium-
high heat, swirling the pan to flavor the oil with the garlic, until the
garlic starts to sizzle but does not color, about 1 minute. Add the bell
peppers, chile, bay leaf, and a generous pinch of salt and stir to coat
the peppers and chile well with the oil. Add ¼ cup (2 fl oz/60 ml)
water and bring to a boil. Reduce the heat to medium-low, cover, and
sweat the peppers and chile until soft and pliable, about 15 minutes.
Meanwhile, in a small bowl, stir together the vinegar and sugar until
the sugar dissolves, then set aside.

Uncover the pan, add the vinegar mixture, raise the heat to high,
and cook until the liquid in the pan has almost evaporated, about
1 minute. Remove from the heat and discard the bay leaf and, if
desired, the garlic. Transfer to a serving dish and serve warm or
at room temperature.

SERVES 4–6

SHORTCUT POLENTA *with* PARMESAN

Unsalted butter for the baking dish and parchment paper

2½ cups (20 fl oz/625 ml) whole milk

Salt

1 cup (5 oz/155 g) coarse-grind yellow polenta

½ cup (4 fl oz/125 ml) heavy cream

1 cup (4 oz/125 g) freshly shredded Parmesan or Asiago cheese

Chopped fresh flat-leaf Italian parsley leaves, for garnish (optional)

Preheat the oven to 350°F (180°C). Generously butter the bottom and sides of an 8-inch (20-cm) square baking dish. Cut an 8-inch (20-cm) square of parchment paper.

In a large saucepan, combine the milk, 2½ cups (20 fl oz/625 ml) water, and 1 tsp salt over medium-high heat. When small bubbles begin to appear around the edge of the pan and the liquid is steaming, slowly pour in the polenta while whisking constantly. When the mixture starts to boil, adjust the heat to keep the mixture at a steady, but not volcanic, boil. Continue to whisk until the mixture thickens to a porridge-like consistency and big bubbles are breaking on the surface, 6–8 minutes.

Pour the polenta into the prepared baking dish. Generously butter one side of the parchment square and place the square, buttered side down, on the surface of the polenta, pressing down gently. Bake for 25 minutes, then remove from the oven.

Peel off the parchment, pour the cream evenly over the surface of the polenta, and then sprinkle with the cheese. With a spoon, gently mix in the cream and cheese until melted, working the spoon around the edge of the dish to incorporate all of the polenta. Season to taste with salt. Ladle into warmed bowls, sprinkle with parsley, if using, and serve right away.

SERVES 4

Polenta comes in various grinds and can be white or yellow, though coarsely ground yellow polenta is the most traditional. You can use any grind here—even stone-ground yellow grits—but do reach for yellow over white. This side dish is also good for breakfast, without the cheese and with a topping of honey or maple syrup.

RADICCHIO

Rocket-shaped Treviso radicchio is a great choice for this dish, but round Chioggia radicchio also works well and is easier to find. Like all chicories, radicchio gets much sweeter when cooked. If you're planning ahead, the croutons and salsa can be made up to 1 day in advance. Store the croutons in a sealed plastic bag at room temperature. Cover the salsa with plastic wrap and refrigerate. Bring to room temperature before serving.

PAN-GRILLED RADICCHIO *with* OLIVE-CAPER SALSA *and* TORN CROUTONS

1 baguette, ½ lb (250 g), halved lengthwise, then torn into 2-inch (5-cm) chunks

½ cup (4 fl oz/125 ml) extra-virgin olive oil, plus more for drizzling

Salt

1 cup (1½ oz/45 g) firmly packed fresh flat-leaf Italian parsley leaves

¼ cup (1¼ oz/35 g) pitted Kalamata olives

¼ cup (1¼ oz/35 g) small pimiento-stuffed green olives

1 tbsp drained capers

1 tbsp finely chopped shallot

4 heads Treviso or round radicchio, about 1½ lb (750 g) total weight

To make the croutons, preheat the oven to 375°F (190°C). Put the baguette chunks in a bowl, drizzle with a little olive oil, sprinkle with salt to taste, and toss to coat the bread evenly. Spread the bread on a rimmed baking sheet and toast until golden brown, about 10 minutes. Let cool.

To make the salsa, in a food processor, combine the parsley, olives, capers, and shallot and pulse until finely chopped. Transfer to a bowl and stir in all but 1 tbsp of the ½ cup (4 fl oz/125 ml) oil.

Remove any discolored or wilted outer leaves from the radicchio. If using round radicchio, cut into thick wedges. If using Treviso, cut in half lengthwise. Arrange the pieces, cut side up, on a rimmed baking sheet, and brush with the remaining 1 tbsp oil.

Heat a ridged grill pan over medium-high heat. Place the radicchio, cut side down, on the hot surface and cook, turning once, until wilted and slightly browned, about 2 minutes on each side.

Arrange the radicchio on a platter, spoon the salsa evenly over the top, then finish with the croutons. Serve warm.

SERVES 4

SMASHED POTATOES
with PAPRIKA SALT

2 lb (1 kg) small red or Yukon gold potatoes	1 tsp fine sea salt
	1 tsp sweet paprika
Salt	½ tsp smoked paprika (pimentón)
3 tbsp olive oil	

Preheat the oven to 400°F (200°C) oven. Line a rimmed baking sheet with parchment paper.

In a large saucepan, combine the potatoes and water to cover by 2 inches (5 cm). Salt the water generously, bring to a boil over high heat, and cook, uncovered, until the potatoes are just tender when pierced with a knife, 12–15 minutes.

While the potatoes are cooking, in a small bowl, stir together the sea salt, sweet paprika, and smoked paprika.

Drain the potatoes in a colander and transfer them to a bowl. Drizzle with 2 tbsp of the olive oil, sprinkle with the paprika salt, and toss until the potatoes are evenly coated. Spread the potatoes in a single layer on the prepared baking sheet. Using the heel of your hand or the back of a wooden spoon, smash each potato until it splits and flattens slightly. Pour the remaining 1 tbsp oil into the bowl used to season the potatoes and stir to mix it with the spices left in the bowl. Brush the mixture over the tops of the smashed potatoes.

Roast the potatoes until the skins are crisp, about 35 minutes. Serve right away.

SERVES 4

Don't be tempted to mash waxy, low-starch red and yellow potatoes, as they'll get sticky. Smash them instead. That way, the insides will stay creamy while the skins get crackly. If you don't like—or don't have—smoked paprika, increase the sweet paprika to 1½ teaspoons.

This dish is quick to make because it calls for basmati rice, which cooks with less liquid and in less time than brown rice or most white varieties. Plus, it has a nutty fragrance and flavor that goes well with sweet onions. Be sure to rinse the rice first to remove the surface starch.

GOLDEN PILAF
with SWEET ONIONS

1 cup (7 oz/220 g) basmati rice

3 tbsp unsalted butter

2 tbsp olive oil

2 large yellow onions, 1 chopped and 1 thinly sliced

Salt

¼ tsp saffron threads, crumbled

1½ cups (12 fl oz/375 ml) low-sodium vegetable or chicken broth

Put the rice in a fine-mesh sieve, rinse under cold running water, and shake dry. In a saucepan, combine 1 tbsp each of the butter and oil over medium-high heat. When the butter melts, add the chopped onion and sauté until very soft, about 4 minutes. Add the rice, ½ tsp salt, and the saffron and stir until the rice is coated, about 30 seconds. Pour in the broth and bring to a boil. Reduce the heat to low, cover, and simmer for 15 minutes. Remove from the heat and let stand, covered, for 10 minutes.

Meanwhile, in a large sauté pan, combine the remaining 2 tbsp butter and 1 tbsp oil over medium-high heat. When the butter melts, add the sliced onion and a pinch of salt and sauté until soft, about 2 minutes. Reduce the heat to low, cover, and sweat the onion until very soft and golden, about 15 minutes. Uncover, raise the heat to high, and stir until the onion turns deep golden brown, about 5 minutes. Be careful it does not scorch.

Uncover the rice and, using a fork, stir in the sliced onion, fluffing the rice and being careful to incorporate all the grains from the bottom of the pan. Transfer to a warmed serving dish or individual plates and serve right away.

SERVES 4

BAKED MASHED POTATOES

4 tbsp (2 oz/60 g) unsalted butter, plus more for the baking dish

4 lb (2 kg) russet potatoes, peeled and cut into large chunks

Salt

4 green onions, halved lengthwise, then thinly sliced crosswise

½ cup (4 fl oz/125 ml) low-sodium vegetable or chicken broth

2 cups (1 lb/500 g) full-fat sour cream

1 cup (4 oz/125 g) grated sharp Cheddar cheese

Preheat the oven to 350°F (180°F). Butter the bottom and sides of a 3-qt (3-l) baking dish.

In a large pot, combine the potatoes and water to cover by 2 inches (5 cm). Salt the water generously, bring to a boil over high heat, and cook, uncovered, until tender all the way through when pierced with a knife, 20–30 minutes, depending on the size of the chunks. Drain in a colander and leave in the sink for 5 minutes to evaporate excess water and steam; do not wash the pot. Pass the potatoes through a ricer into a large bowl. Set aside.

In the same pot, melt the butter over medium heat. Add the green onions and sauté until softened, about 1 minute. Pour in the broth. Pour the broth mixture over the potatoes, then, using a rubber spatula, fold the sour cream into the potatoes until evenly blended. Season the potatoes with salt and spread them in the prepared baking dish. (At this point, the potatoes can be covered and refrigerated for up to 8 hours. Let come to room temperature before baking.)

Sprinkle the cheese evenly over the potatoes. Bake until the cheese is melted and crusty at the edges, about 30 minutes. Let stand for about 5 minutes, then serve.

SERVES 8–10

RUSSET POTATOES

In the wide world of potatoes, the best for mashed is still the unsexy russet, sometimes labeled "Idaho" in markets, due to its starchy flesh. For maximum fluffiness, use a ricer: a perforated pot-shaped utensil with a rim-attached plunger for forcing the potatoes through the holes. If you lack a ricer, use a stand mixer fitted with the paddle attachment.

The snap in these peas is in their crunchy edible pods. Although the newest hybrids are mostly string-free, when you snap off the stem end of each one, it's a good idea to pull downward along its inside curve to check for tough strings. Make sure the peas are completely dry before you begin cooking or the oil will splatter when they hit the pan.

STIR-FRIED SNAP PEAS *with* ALMONDS, MAPLE, *and* SOY

2 tbsp canola or grapeseed oil

⅓ cup (1½ oz/45 g) slivered blanched almonds

Salt

1 lb (500 g) sugar snap peas, trimmed

2 tbsp reduced-sodium soy sauce

1 tbsp maple syrup, preferably grade B

Pinch of cayenne pepper

1 tsp grated lemon zest

Place a large sauté pan or wok over medium-high heat. When the pan is hot, pour in 1 tbsp of the oil and tilt the pan to coat it with the oil. Add the almonds and a pinch of salt and stir-fry until the almonds turn golden and smell toasty, about 45 seconds. Using a slotted spoon, transfer the almonds to a plate and set aside.

Return the pan to high heat. When hot, add the remaining 1 tbsp oil, tilt the pan again to coat it, and then add the snap peas and stir-fry until glossy and starting to blister in spots, about 1 minute. Pour in ⅓ cup (3 fl oz/80 ml) water, stir once, cover, and reduce the heat to medium. Let the snap peas steam until tender-crisp, about 3 minutes.

Uncover, raise the heat to high, and stir in the soy sauce, maple syrup, and cayenne pepper. Stir-fry until the snap peas are glazed with the sauce, about 1 minute more. Remove from the heat and stir in the lemon zest and reserved almonds. Transfer to a warmed serving dish and serve right away.

SERVES 4

STEAK HOUSE SPINACH

1 lb (500 g) baby spinach leaves	1 lemon
2 tbsp unsalted butter	Pinch of freshly grated nutmeg
3 green onions, thinly sliced	Salt and freshly ground pepper
¼ lb (125 g) cream cheese, at room temperature, cut into small pieces	

Rinse the spinach well and shake dry, leaving a little water clinging to the leaves.

In a large sauté pan, melt the butter over medium heat. Add the green onions and sauté until soft, about 2 minutes. Add half of the spinach, cover the pan, and let the spinach cook down, about 1 minute. Add the remaining spinach, re-cover the pan, and let it cook down, about 1 minute.

Remove the pan from the heat. Using a slotted spoon transfer the spinach to a food processor, and pulse until finely chopped. (At this point, the spinach can be cooled, covered, and refrigerated for up to 1 day before continuing.)

Return the spinach to the pan and place over medium heat. Stir in the cream cheese, a piece or two at a time, until bubbly and blended with the spinach. Grate the zest of the lemon directly into the pan, then halve the lemon and squeeze in about 1 tsp of the juice. Season with the nutmeg, salt, and pepper, taste and adjust with more lemon juice if needed, then transfer to a warmed serving dish and serve right away.

SERVES 2–4

Once upon a time, the only spinach in the market were big bunches of muddy leaves or frozen spinach with mushy texture. Now, there are bins overflowing with tender, emerald-green baby spinach that is much easier to manage. Even though baby spinach is often labeled "prewashed," always give it a good rinse before using.

*It's not really summer
without zucchini on
the dinner table. For
this recipe, look for both
green and yellow ones
and their pals from
the squash patch, such
as yellow crookneck
and straightneck.
Select squashes that are
6–8 inches (15–20 cm)
long. Once they've grown
to the size of a rolling
pin, they are too bitter
for this dish.*

GRILLED SUMMER SQUASH
with PINE NUT PICADA

6 tbsp (3 fl oz/90 ml) extra-virgin olive oil, plus more for brushing

2 lb (1 kg) assorted summer squashes, cut lengthwise into slices ½ inch (12 mm) thick

Salt

¼ cup (1¼ oz/35 g) pine nuts

2 cloves garlic, minced

⅓ cup (⅔ oz/20 g) panko

½ tsp red pepper flakes

2 tbsp sherry vinegar

2 tbsp minced fresh oregano

¼ cup (⅓ oz/10 g) minced fresh flat-leaf parsley leaves

Prepare a medium-hot fire in a charcoal or gas grill. Brush a rimmed baking sheet with oil.

Brush the squash slices on both sides with oil and then sprinkle all over with salt. Grill the squash, turning once, until slightly charred but not blackened, about 4 minutes on each side. Transfer the squash slices to the prepared baking sheet.

In a dry nonstick skillet, toast the pine nuts over medium heat, shaking the pan often, until they are golden and smell toasty, about 2 minutes. Pour into a bowl. Return the pan to medium-high heat and add 3 tbsp of the oil. When the oil is hot, add the garlic, and sauté until fragrant, about 30 seconds. Add the panko and pepper flakes and stir until the panko is toasted, about 1 minute. Scrape the panko into the bowl with the pine nuts and toss to mix.

In a small bowl, stir together the remaining 3 tbsp oil, the vinegar, the oregano, the parsley, and a pinch of salt. Place the grilled squash on a platter and spoon the vinegar-parsley mixture over the top. Sprinkle with the pine nut mixture and serve right away.

SERVES 4–6

Sweet Potato Gratin
with Sage Cream

Unsalted butter for the baking dish	1 cup low-sodium vegetable or chicken broth
½ cup (2 oz/60 g) freshly shredded Parmesan cheese	2 cloves garlic, mashed
½ cup (2 oz/60 g) shredded Gruyère cheese	4 fresh sage leaves, torn in half
	Salt and freshly grated pepper
1 cup (8 fl oz/250 ml) heavy cream	2 lb (1 kg) Garnet sweet potatoes
	2 russet potatoes

When is a yam not a yam? When it's a sweet potato, which is the botanical truth about dark-skinned, orange-fleshed Garnet sweet potatoes that many markets label "yams." By alternating Garnets with russet potatoes, you keep this holiday classic from being too cloying.

Preheat the oven to 375°F (190°C). Grease the bottom and sides of a 9-by-13-inch (23-by-33-cm) or similar 3-qt (3-l) baking dish with butter. In a small bowl, toss together the Parmesan and Gruyère cheeses.

In a small saucepan, combine the cream, broth, garlic, sage, and a good pinch of salt over medium-low heat and heat until small bubbles begin to appear around the edge of the pan and the liquid is steaming. Remove from the heat and let steep while you prepare the potatoes.

Cut the rounded ends off of each potato, then peel the potatoes. Using a food processor or mandoline fitted with the slicing blade, cut the potatoes crosswise into slices ¼ inch (6 mm) thick. Layer the potato slices, alternating types, in the prepared baking dish. Pour the warm cream mixture through a fine-mesh sieve evenly over the potatoes and discard the garlic and sage. Cover the dish tightly with foil and bake for 45 minutes.

Uncover and sprinkle the potatoes with the cheeses. Continue to bake, uncovered, until the mixture is bubbly and thick, 25–30 minutes. Let stand for 10 minutes before serving.

SERVES 6–8

This is a golden age for tomatoes, and this dish is a great way to celebrate the bounty. Choose ripe, fragrant tomatoes in as many different colors as you can—red, orange, gold, purple, green, even striped—for this warm and cold, crunchy and soft spin on Italian bread salad.

HEIRLOOM TOMATO PANZANELLA *with* BURRATA

2 pt (1¼ lb/625 g) cherry tomatoes, stemmed

Extra-virgin olive oil

Coarse sea salt

½ tsp red pepper flakes

3 slices crusty bread such as ciabatta, each about 1 inch (2.5 cm) thick, torn into small pieces

2 lb (1 kg) heirloom tomatoes, in assorted colors and sizes, cored

¼ lb (125 g) burrata cheese

About 2 tbsp prepared basil pesto

1 tbsp red wine vinegar

Position 2 racks in the center of the oven and preheat to 375°F (190°C). Line 2 rimmed baking sheets with parchment paper.

Halve the cherry tomatoes and put them in a bowl. Add 1 tbsp oil, ½ tsp salt, and the pepper flakes and toss to coat the tomatoes evenly. Spread the cherry tomatoes on 1 prepared baking sheet and bake, turning them over with a spatula halfway through the cooking time, until soft and slightly caramelized, 25–30 minutes.

Put the bread in a bowl, drizzle with about 2 tbsp oil and sprinkle with salt to taste, then toss to coat evenly. Spread the bread on the second prepared baking sheet, place in the oven alongside the tomatoes, and toast until golden brown and crisp, 20–25 minutes.

Meanwhile, slice some of the heirloom tomatoes and cut the remainder into wedges, to create a variety of shapes and sizes. Scatter them on a serving platter. Tear the cheese into small pieces and scatter over the heirloom tomatoes. Dollop small drops of pesto evenly over the tomatoes and cheese, then scatter the warm cherry tomatoes over the top. Sprinkle everything with the vinegar and a pinch of salt. Strew the croutons over the tomatoes and cheese, drizzle a little more oil over the top, and serve right away.

SERVES 4–6

BUTTER-BRAISED TURNIPS *with* CARAWAY

2 lb (1 kg) small turnips

2 tbsp unsalted butter

Salt

¼ cup (2 fl oz/60 ml) low-sodium vegetable or chicken broth or water

¼ tsp caraway seeds

To peel the turnips, cut off the greens if still attached, then cut a thin slice off both ends of each turnip to expose the flesh. Stand a turnip on one flat end and slice off the peel all the way around, cutting from the top to the bottom. Cut the turnip in half vertically, then cut each half into wedges ½ inch (12 mm) thick. Repeat with the remaining turnips.

In a large sauté pan, melt the butter over medium-high heat. When the foam subsides, add the turnips and sprinkle them with salt. Sauté for 1 minute, then pour in the broth and let come to a boil. Reduce the heat to medium-low, cover, and simmer the turnips until just tender when pierced with a knife, 12–15 minutes.

Uncover and raise the heat to high. Cook, shaking the pan, until the liquid evaporates and the turnips are glazed with the pan juices, about 3 minutes. Stir in the caraway seeds, season with salt, and transfer to a warmed serving dish. Serve right away.

SERVES 4

All in the family, that's what root vegetables such as turnips, rutabagas, and radishes are, and they can all be braised and used interchangeably in this dish (radishes don't need to be peeled). Look for small turnips, which have the best flavor and texture, with the tops attached for maximum freshness. Save the greens for sautéing as you would spinach or Swiss chard.

WINTER SQUASH

Here's how to tackle a butternut squash: using a chef's knife, cut the skinny, straight "neck" off the bulb, halve both sections lengthwise, discard the seeds from the bulb section, then peel both sections and cut the flesh into cubes. Or, you can cheat: it's easy to find precut squash in the produce section.

BUTTERNUT SQUASH PUREE *with* BROWN BUTTER *and* SAGE

3 generous cups (1 lb/500 g) peeled and cubed butternut squash (2½-inch/6-cm cubes)

3 tbsp unsalted butter

½ cup (2 fl oz/60 ml) vegetable or chicken broth or water

Salt

1 tbsp chopped fresh sage

In a large saucepan, combine the squash cubes, 1 tbsp butter, the broth, and a generous pinch of salt over high heat. When the liquid comes to a boil, stir well so the butter melts into the liquid. Cover, reduce the heat to medium-low, and cook until the squash collapses when pushed with a spoon, about 15 minutes.

Uncover and stir the squash vigorously with a wooden spoon until it is lightly mashed and the liquid in the pan has been absorbed. Remove from the heat, re-cover the pan, and set aside. (At this point, the squash can sit in the pan for up to 1 hour. Reheat over a low heat, stirring until heated through and adding a bit more broth or water if the mixture has become too dense.)

In a very small pan, melt the remaining 2 tbsp butter over medium heat. When the foam subsides, add the sage and reduce the heat to low. Cook, uncovered, until the butter turns nut brown and smells fragrant and the sage is dark green and crisp, 3–4 minutes.

Pour the butter and sage over the squash in the large pan and, with a sturdy whisk, whip the mixture until creamy and light. Season with salt, transfer to a warmed serving dish, and serve right away.

SERVES 4

Side Dishes Pairings

This...	Goes with That	This...	Goes with That
Braised Artichokes with Mint	grilled lamb chops	Fava Bean and Celery Salad with Ricotta Salata	grilled tuna or swordfish
Arugula Salad with Pomegranates and Pistachios	roast beef, turkey, or chicken	Caramelized Fennel with Shallots and Olives	grilled shrimp or scallops
Asparagus with Hazelnut Gremolata	roast leg of lamb, salmon	Slow-Cooked Greek-Style Green Beans	rack of lamb, lamb shanks
Golden Flannel Hash	pot roast, poached eggs	Crunchy Kale Slaw with Radishes	carnitas
Roasted Broccoli with Parmesan and Pepper Flakes	roast chicken, fish	Mixed-Mushroom Compotes	prime rib, beef fillet
Spicy Broccoli Rabe with Anchovy and Preserved Lemon	roast fish, pasta	Onion and Leek Panades	veal chops
Roasted Brussels Sprouts with Bacon-Walnut Vinaigrette	roast turkey, pork	Parsnip and Carrot Latkes	brisket
Bulgur and Lentil Pilaf with Toasted Cashews	short ribs, lamb stew	Sweet and Hot Peperonata	grilled sausages
Warm Red Cabbage Salad with Goat Cheese	pork chops, turkey burgers	Shortcut Polenta with Parmesan	Bolognese sauce, meatballs
Sweet-Hot Roasted Carrots	fish, roast chicken	Pan-Grilled Radicchio with Olive-Caper Salsa and Torn Croutons	grilled rib eye, salmon
Curried Roasted Cauliflower	lamb stew, roast chicken	Smashed Potatoes with Paprika Salt	roast beef, brisket
Celery and Apple Stuffing	roast turkey	Golden Pilaf with Sweet Onions	braised chicken, beef stew
Celery Root Rémoulade	grilled cheese sandwiches	Baked Mashed Potatoes	roast turkey
Swiss Chard with Currants and Pine Nuts	grilled steaks, pork chops	Stir-Fried Snap Peas with Almonds, Maple, and Soy	chicken or turkey cutlets
Creamed Corn with Chipotle and Queso Fresco	hamburgers, tacos	Steak House Spinach	T-bone, skirt steak
Spiced Couscous	braised chicken, lamb	Grilled Summer Squash with Pine Nut Picada	grilled salmon or sausages
Braised Moroccan Eggplant	lamb chops, fish	Sweet Potato Gratin with Sage Cream	roast turkey
Roasted Endive with Prosciutto	pork tenderloin	Heirloom Tomato Panzanella with Burrata	grilled chicken, flank steak
English Pea and Onion Gratin	leg of lamb, roast turkey	Butter-Braised Turnips with Caraway	pork tenderloin, ham
Farro with Winter Squash and Pecans	roast chicken	Butternut Squash Puree with Brown Butter and Sage	roast beef, roast turkey, ham

Index

weldonowen

1045 Sansome Street, Suite 100, San Francisco, CA 94111

www.weldonowen.com

Weldon Owen is a division of

BONNIER

WELDON OWEN, INC.

President & Publisher Roger Shaw
SVP, Sales & Marketing Amy Kaneko
Finance Manager Philip Paulick

Associate Publisher Jennifer Newens
Associate Editor Emma Rudolph

Creative Director Kelly Booth
Art Director Alisha Petro
Senior Production Designer Rachel Lopez Metzger

Production Director Chris Hemesath
Associate Production Director Michelle Duggan

Photographer Katie Newburn
Food Stylist Erin Quon
Prop Stylist Glenn Jenkins
Illustrator Margaret Berg

THE SIDE DISH HANDBOOK

Conceived and produced by Weldon Owen, Inc.
Copyright © 2014 Weldon Owen, Inc.

Printed and bound by 1010 Printing, Ltd. in China

First printed in 2014
10 9 8 7 6 5 4 3 2

Library of Congress Control Number: 2014943528

ISBN-13: 978-1-61628-813-6
ISBN-10: 1-61628-813-2

ACKNOWLEDGMENTS

Weldon Owen wishes to thank the following people for their
generous support in producing this book: Alexa Hyman, Kim Laidlaw,
Daniel Dent, Elizabeth Parson, and Sharon Silva